TRINITY
COLLEGE LONDON PRESS

ROCK & POP

GRADE

03
VOCALS

Published by
Trinity College London Press Ltd
trinitycollege.com

Registered in England
Company no. 09726123

Photography by Zute Lightfoot, lightfootphoto.com

© Copyright 2017 Trinity College London Press Ltd
Fourth impression, January 2023

Printed in England by Caligraving Ltd

Parental and Teacher Guidance:

The songs in Trinity's Rock & Pop syllabus have been arranged
to represent the artists' original recordings as closely and
authentically as possible. Popular music frequently deals with
subject matter that some may find offensive or challenging.
It is possible that the songs may include material that some
might find unsuitable for use with younger learners.

We recommend that parents and teachers exercise their own
judgement to satisfy themselves that the lyrics of selected
songs are appropriate for the students concerned. As you
will be aware, there is no requirement that all songs in this
syllabus must be learned. Trinity does not associate itself with,
adopt or endorse any of the opinions or views expressed in
the selected songs.

THE EXAM AT A GLANCE

In your exam you will perform a set of three songs and one of the session skills assessments. You can choose the order of your set list.

SONG 1

Choose a song from this book.

SONG 2

Choose *either* a different song from this book
or a song from the list of additional Trinity Rock & Pop arrangements, available at trinityrock.com
or a song you have chosen yourself: this could be your own cover version or a song that you have written. It should be at the same level as the songs in this book and match the parameters at trinityrock.com

SONG 3: TECHNICAL FOCUS

Song 3 is designed to help you develop specific and relevant techniques in performance. Choose one of the technical focus songs from this book, which cover two specific technical elements.

SESSION SKILLS

Choose *either* **playback** *or* **improvising**.

Session skills are an essential part of every Rock & Pop exam. They are designed to help you develop the techniques music industry performers need.

Sample tests are available in our *Session Skills* books and free examples can be downloaded from trinityrock.com

ACCESS ALL AREAS

GET THE FULL ROCK & POP EXPERIENCE ONLINE AT TRINITYROCK.COM

We have created a range of digital resources to support your learning and give you insider information from the music industry, available online. You will find support, advice and digital content on:

- Songs, performance and technique
- Session skills
- The music industry

You can access tips and tricks from industry professionals featuring:

- Bite-sized videos that include tips from professional musicians on techniques used in the songs
- 'Producer's notes' on the tracks, to increase your knowledge of rock and pop
- Blog posts on performance tips, musical styles, developing technique and advice from the music industry

JOIN US ONLINE AT:

 /TRINITYROCKANDPOP    @TRINITY_ROCK    /TRINITYROCKANDPOP   and at **TRINITYROCK.COM**

CONTENTS

THE AUDIO

Professional demo & backing tracks can be downloaded free, see inside cover for details.

Music preparation and book layout by Andrew Skirrow for Camden Music Services
Music consultants: Nick Crispin, Chris Walters, Christopher Hussey, Donna Rudd
Audio arranged, recorded & produced by Tom Fleming
Vocal arrangements by Jane Watkins & Christopher Hussey

Musicians
Bass: Tom Fleming, Ben Heartland
Drums: George Double
Guitar: Tom Fleming
Vocals: Bo Walton, Alison Symons, Emily Barden

YOUR
PAGE
NOTES

ADVENTURE OF A LIFETIME
COLDPLAY

**WORDS AND MUSIC: GUY BERRYMAN, JONNY BUCKLAND
WILL CHAMPION, MIKKEL S. ERIKSEN
TOR ERIK HERMANSEN, CHRIS MARTIN**

SINGLE BY
Coldplay

ALBUM
A Head Full Of Dreams

RELEASED
6 November 2015

RECORDED
**1 March 2014-
22 August 2015
Henson Recording Studio
Los Angeles, California USA
AIR Studios, London
England
The Bakery, London
England
The Beehive, London
England (album)**

LABEL
Parlophone

WRITERS
**Guy Berryman
Jonny Buckland
Will Champion
Mikkel S. Eriksen
Tor Erik Hermansen
Chris Martin**

PRODUCERS
**Rik Simpson
Stargate**

Formed in London, England in 1996 by Chris Martin (vocals, piano, acoustic guitar), Jonny Buckland (guitar), Guy Berryman (bass) and Will Champion (drums), Coldplay are the most successful band to emerge from England in the 21st century with global sales of over 80 million.

The lead single from Coldplay's seventh consecutive UK No. 1 studio album *A Head Full of Dreams*, 'Adventure of a Lifetime' was written by the band with (and produced by) the Norwegian duo Stargate, who had previously written and produced No. 1 hits for Rihanna, Beyoncé, Shakira, Ne-Yo, Wiz Khalifa and Hear'Say. About Stargate's contribution, Buckland said:

> They'd always come back with something interesting, something we'd never come up with.

Speaking about the song's starting point, Martin revealed:

> I was asking the rest of the band to start something to see if a song comes out of it, so not everything comes from me. It came from Jonny's riff. I'd been begging Jonny for years to make a riff that I like as much as 'Sweet Child o' Mine' by Guns N' Roses, then he showed me that one, and I was like, that's it!

The single became Coldplay's 16th top-ten hit in the UK.

⚡ PERFORMANCE TIPS

The rhythm of this song includes semiquavers and syncopation, requiring attention to detail. Several phrases begin on off-beats and late into bars, so count these passages carefully. The phrases are also quite broken up, so you'll need to create a sense of continuity in your performance to compensate for the frequent rests. The very first note is the ninth of the chord (F sharp over E minor) so you'll need to pitch this confidently.

ADVENTURE OF A LIFETIME

WORDS AND MUSIC:
GUY BERRYMAN, JONNY BUCKLAND,
WILL CHAMPION, MIKKEL S. ERIKSEN,
TOR ERIK HERMANSEN, CHRIS MARTIN

SINGLE BY
Pretenders

ALBUM
Pretenders

B-SIDE
**Swinging London
Nervous But Shy**

RELEASED
November 1979

RECORDED
**1979, Wessex Studios,
London, England
AIR Studios, London,
England (album)**

LABEL
Real Records

WRITERS
**Chrissie Hynde
James Honeyman-Scott**

PRODUCER
Chris Thomas

TECHNICAL FOCUS

BRASS IN POCKET PRETENDERS

WORDS AND MUSIC: CHRISSIE HYNDE, JAMES HONEYMAN-SCOTT

Pretenders were formed in 1978 by American musician Chrissie Hynde (vocals, guitar) with English musicians James Honeyman-Scott (guitar, keyboards), Pete Farndon (bass) and Martin Chambers (drums), a line-up that would last until 1982. Thirteen of the band's albums have made the UK top 40, from their 1980 self-titled debut to 2016's *Alone*.

Pretenders' third single 'Brass in Pocket' was released at the beginning of November 1979. By the middle of January 1980 it had replaced Pink Floyd's 'Another Brick in the Wall (Part II)' at the top of the UK singles chart to become the first new No. 1 of the 1980s. In 2004, Hynde said:

> When we recorded the song I wasn't very happy with it and told my producer that he could release it over my dead body, but they eventually persuaded me. So I remember feeling a bit sheepish when it went to No. 1.

The song also made it to No. 14 on the Billboard Hot 100, making it the band's first US hit.

TECHNICAL FOCUS

Two technical focus elements are featured in this song:

- Power across a wide range
- Bends

This upbeat song makes a feature of **bends**, beginning at bar 19. These should have a squeal-like quality, so take the pitch as high as you can manage, listening to the original version for guidance. You'll also need to show **power across a wide range**, a good example of which is the section at bars 26-29. The octave leaps here and the descending phrase to low A should all sound equally strong, wherever in your voice you are singing.

BRASS IN POCKET

WORDS AND MUSIC:
CHRISSIE HYNDE, JAMES HONEYMAN-SCOTT

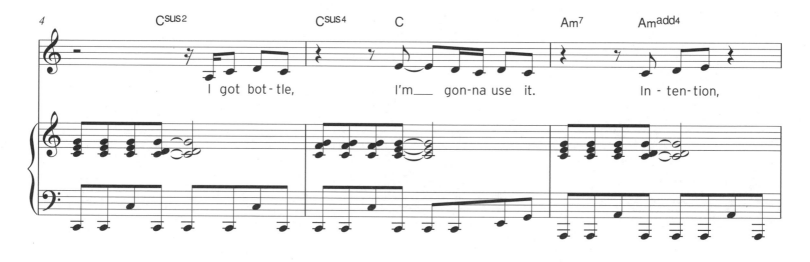

SINGLE BY
Norah Jones

ALBUM
Come Away With Me

RELEASED
**26 February 2002
(album)
July 2002 (single)**

LABEL
Blue Note

WRITER
Jesse Harris

PRODUCERS
**Norah Jones
Arif Mardin
Jay Newland**

DON'T KNOW WHY
NORAH JONES

WORDS AND MUSIC: JESSE HARRIS

Norah Jones was born Geetali Norah Shankar in Brooklyn on March 30th, 1979, daughter of the Indian sitar virtuoso Ravi Shankar. She studied jazz piano at the University of North Texas before moving back to New York City and signing to the legendary jazz label Blue Note in 2001.

'Don't Know Why' was written by songwriter Jesse Harris and originally appeared on his second album, released in 1999. Harris contributed this and four more songs to Jones' 2002 debut album, *Come Away with Me*, one of which he co-wrote with Jones, as well as playing guitar on seven of its 14 tracks (including 'Don't Know Why'). Recorded when she was just 21 years old, Jones's debut was produced by industry veteran Arif Mardin and released in 2002 with 'Don't Know Why' as its first single. The album climbed to No. 1 almost a year after its release in January 2003, going on to sell over 26 million copies and topping the charts worldwide. It won eight Grammys, including Album of the Year and Best Female Pop Vocal Performance.

 ## PERFORMANCE TIPS

This song is all about creating a smooth, relaxed and tender atmosphere, so aim to capture these qualities in your vocal. There are pitching challenges too, namely the repeated use of the note A to begin phrases over a B flat major seventh chord. This chord means that the A is technically a harmony note, but it's still a dissonance with the B flat, requiring care. Look out too for occasional wide leaps in the melody.

DON'T KNOW WHY

WORDS AND MUSIC: JESSE HARRIS

SINGLE BY
Coldplay

ALBUM
Parachutes

B-SIDE
**Help Is Round the Corner
No More Keeping My Feet
on the Ground**

RELEASED
26 June 2000

RECORDED
**March 2000
Rockfield Studios
in Monmouth**

LABEL
Parlophone

WRITERS
**Chris Martin
Jonny Buckland
Guy Berryman
Will Champion
Andre Benz**

PRODUCERS
**ken Nelson
Coldplay**

TECHNICAL FOCUS

YELLOW
COLDPLAY

WORDS AND MUSIC: GUY BERRYMAN, JON BUCKLAND, WILL CHAMPION, CHRIS MARTIN

English group Coldplay are one of the most successful bands to emerge in the 21st century. The quartet of Chris Martin, Jonny Buckland, Guy Berryman and Will Champion have topped the UK albums chart with all seven of their studio albums and have headlined the Glastonbury Festival more times than any other act, achieving their record-breaking fourth headline visit in 2016.

'Yellow' was Coldplay's breakthrough single, released in 2000, two weeks before their debut album *Parachutes*. A lovelorn, anthemic classic, the song was written during recording sessions for the album following the completion of its lead single 'Shiver'. 'Yellow' reached No. 4 in the UK singles chart, won Best Single at the 2001 NME Awards and was nominated for two Brit Awards and two Grammy Awards. Meanwhile, *Parachutes* won a Best British Album Brit Award and Best Alternative Music Album Grammy Award. It was the first of many top-10 UK hits for the band, numbering 17 by 2016.

TECHNICAL FOCUS

Two technical focus elements are featured in this song:

- Interval leaps
- Syncopation

There are several challenging **interval leaps** in this song that will require careful pitching. Pay particular attention to the ascending major 6th and the descending perfect 5th that first appear in bars 23-24. Aim to sing these intervals precisely while keeping an even and controlled tone. **Syncopation** is a strong feature of 'Yellow' and careful practice is needed to achieve a precise but natural effect. Look carefully at where the words are placed, particularly in bars 10, 16 and 34, and use the text to help you shape the rhythm. Try clapping the pulse and saying the words in rhythm to help you put them together.

YELLOW

WORDS AND MUSIC:
GUY BERRYMAN, JON BUCKLAND,
WILL CHAMPION, CHRIS MARTIN

Rock ♩ = 87 (2 bars count-in)

SINGLE BY
Lou Reed

ALBUM
Transformer

A-SIDE
Walk On The Wild Side

RELEASED
8 November 1972 (album)
17 November 1972
(single)

RECORDED
31 August 1972
Trident Studios, London,
England

LABEL
RCA

WRITER
Lou Reed

PRODUCERS
David Bowie
Mick Ronson

TECHNICAL FOCUS

PERFECT DAY
LOU REED

WORDS AND MUSIC: LOU REED

As founding member, chief songwriter and frontman of The Velvet Underground, one of the most influential bands in rock history, Lou Reed cemented his standing as one of rock music's most lyrically gifted and boundary pushing artists. A subsequent 50-year solo career included commercial success with albums such as *Transformer* and divisive experiments such as *Metal Machine Music*.

'Perfect Day' was written for Reed's second solo album, 1972's *Transformer*, which turned him from cult figure to popstar thanks to the international hit 'Walk on the Wild Side'. The album was produced by long-time Velvet Underground fan David Bowie and guitarist Mick Ronson, the latter also writing the string arrangements and playing piano on the album. 'Perfect Day' was introduced to a new generation through its inclusion in the hit 1996 film *Trainspotting*, playing out in its entirety during a single scene. The following year the BBC commissioned a promo clip featuring a star-studded performance of the song, including Reed, Bowie, Elton John, Bono, Tom Jones, Dr John and more. This version proved so popular that the track was released as a charity single for Children in Need. Topping the UK chart for three weeks, it went on to sell over 1.5 million copies.

TECHNICAL FOCUS

Two technical focus elements are featured in this song:

- Pitching
- Style

This song features some chromatic melodic lines that need careful **pitching**, for example bars 4, 8, 18 and 22. The **style** offers a challenge too, with the semi-spoken verse contrasting with the epic singalong quality of the chorus. Both sections need to be delivered with confidence and attention to mood and character.

TECHNICAL FOCUS

PERFECT DAY

WORDS AND MUSIC: LOU REED

then la-ter,___ a mov-ie too, and then home. Oh,

it's such a per-fect day,___ I'm glad I spent it with you.___ Oh, such a per-fect day, you just

keep me hang-ing on,___ you just keep me hang-ing on.___

To Coda

Just a per-fect day, prob-lems all left a-lone,

SINGLE BY
Lorde

ALBUM
Pure Heroine

RELEASED
3 June 2013

RECORDED
2012, Golden Age, Morningside, Auckland, New Zealand

LABEL
Lava Republic

WRITERS
Lorde Joel Little

PRODUCER
Joel Little

ROYALS
LORDE

WORDS AND MUSIC: LORDE, JOEL LITTLE

Born Ella Marija Lani Yelich-O'Connor in Takapuna, New Zealand, Lorde signed to Universal Music in her early teens and released her debut single, 2013's 'Royals', at the age of 16. A huge international hit, the impact of this and her debut album *Pure Heroine* led to her being chosen to curate the soundtrack to the 2014 film *The Hunger Games: Mockingjay Part 1*.

Inspired by the 'unrelatable, unattainable opulence' of many contemporary hip-hop artists' lifestyles, Lorde said of writing 'Royals' that:

> I was just at my house and I wrote it before I went to the studio. I wrote it in, like, half an hour – the lyrics, anyway. I wrote all the lyrics and took them to the studio and my producer [Joel Little] was like, 'Yeah, this is cool.'

Lorde became the youngest solo artist to write and perform a No. 1 hit in the US, where 'Royals' topped the charts for nine consecutive weeks, reached sales in excess of seven million and won the prestigious Song of the Year at the 2014 Grammy Awards.

 ## PERFORMANCE TIPS

The lyrics in this song offer a real challenge, especially from bar 11, requiring clear diction. You'll also need good control of breathing, as there are long phrases to sing and only short rests in which to breath. Try also to capture the stylised feel of this song, delivering the lyrics with poise and control, even at the louder dynamics.

ROYALS

WORDS AND MUSIC:
LORDE, JOEL LITTLE

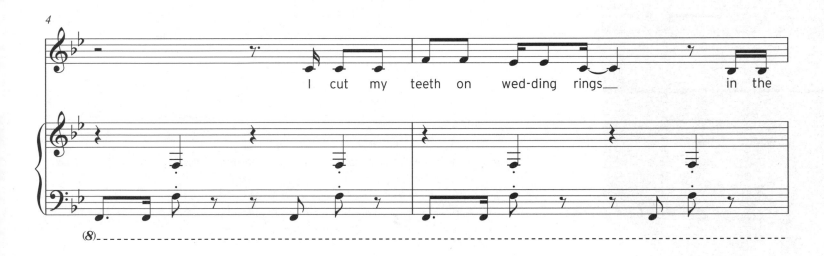

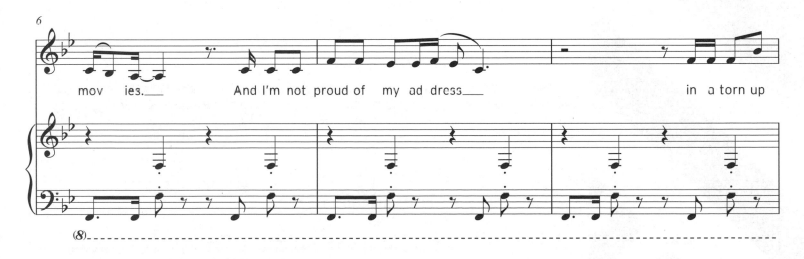

SINGLE BY
Diana Ross

ALBUM
Diana

B-SIDE
Friend To Friend

RELEASED
22 May 1980 (album)
25 June 1980 (single)

RECORDED
December 1979–March 1980

The Power Station, New York City, New York, USA

Electric Lady Studios, New York City, New York, USA

Motown Recording Studios, California, Los Angeles, USA (album)

LABEL
Motown

WRITERS
Bernard Edwards
Nile Rodgers

PRODUCERS
Bernard Edwards
Nile Rodgers

UPSIDE DOWN

DIANA ROSS

WORDS AND MUSIC: BERNARD EDWARDS, NILE RODGERS

Detroit-born Diana Ross found fame as lead singer of The Supremes, Motown's most successful act of the 1960s who achieved 12 No. 1 hits in the US in that decade. She launched her solo career in 1970, scoring the first of six US No. 1s that year to become one of the most successful female singers in music history.

'Upside Down' was the lead single from Ross' tenth solo album, 1980's *Diana*. The whole album was written and produced by Chic's Nile Rodgers and Bernard Edwards, who were riding high from the previous year's US No. 1 'Good Times' and Sister Sledge's *We Are Family* album (which they wrote, produced and played on and had yielded three big hits in 'He's the Greatest Dancer', 'Lost in Music' and the title track). Edwards and Rodgers also play bass and guitar on the album, with their bandmate Tony Thompson on drums, making it for all intents and purposes a Chic album with Ross on vocals. Ross began her third decade in the music business with the biggest single and album of her career, hitting No. 2 on the US album chart and topping the US singles chart for four weeks. The album also produced the US or UK top-five hits 'I'm Coming Out' and 'My Old Piano'.

⚡ PERFORMANCE TIPS

Take care of the rhythm and phrasing in this song – there are plenty of semiquaver and syncopated passages to look out for, and the 'Upside down' lyric will require an emphatic staccato attack. There are occasional complex lyrics that will require close attention to diction, and the $\frac{2}{4}$ bars will need careful counting.

UPSIDE DOWN

WORDS AND MUSIC:
BERNARD EDWARDS, NILE RODGERS

SINGLE BY
Amy Winehouse

ALBUM
Back To Black

B-SIDE
To Know Him Is To Love Him (live)
Monkey Man
You Know I'm No Good (Skeewiff Mix)

RELEASED
27 October 2006 (album)
5 January 2007 (single)

RECORDED
2005-2006
Chung King Studio, New York City, New York, USA
Daptone Studios, Brooklyn, New York, USA
Metropolis Studios, London, England

LABEL
Island

WRITER
Amy Winehouse

PRODUCER
Mark Ronson

YOU KNOW I'M NO GOOD AMY WINEHOUSE

WORDS AND MUSIC: AMY WINEHOUSE

One of the most distinctive and successful singer-songwriters of her generation, Amy Winehouse was born in London, England in 1983. She followed her 2003 debut album *Frank* with 2006's hugely successful and Grammy Award-winning *Back to Black*, a critical and commercial hit that launched her to international stardom but would prove to be her final release.

One of the highlights of Winehouse's *Back to Black*, 'You Know I'm No Good' was released as the second single from the Mark Ronson-produced album after the instant classic 'Rehab'. Both recordings featured many members of Brooklyn funk/soul band The Dap-Kings, including drummer Homer Steinweiss, keyboard player Victor Axelrod, guitarists Binky Griptite and Thomas Brenneck and bandleader/arranger Gabriel Roth. Dap-Kings members also provided the notable brass parts. The album topped the UK album chart on four occasions, becoming the UK's best-selling album of 2007 and returning to the top one final time for three weeks following Winehouse's tragic death in July 2011. It remains the second best-selling album of the 21st century in the UK, only Adele's *21* having outsold it.

 PERFORMANCE TIPS

The melody of this memorable song features plenty of blue notes and inflections. These will require authentic performance to achieve the necessary style and feel. Try to perform the song with a sense of freedom and swagger, which will help you capture the complex but extrovert mood of the music.

YOU KNOW I'M NO GOOD

WORDS AND MUSIC: AMY WINEHOUSE

Meet you down-stairs_ in the bar_ and heard,_ your rolled up sleeves and your

skull T-shirt;_ you say, "What did you do_ with_ him to-day?"_ And

I cheat-ed my-self, like I knew__ I would.

__ I told you I__ was trou-ble;__ you

know that I'm__ no good.__

CHOOSING SONGS FOR YOUR EXAM

SONG 1

Choose a song from this book.

SONG 2

Choose a song which is:

Either a different song from this book

or from the list of additional Trinity Rock & Pop arrangements, available at trinityrock.com

or from a printed or online source

or your own arrangement

or a song that you have written yourself

You can perform Song 2 unaccompanied or with a backing track (minus the voice). If you like, you can create a backing track yourself (or with friends), include a live self-played accompaniment on any instrument, or be accompanied live by another musician.

The level of difficulty and length of the song should be similar to the songs in this book and match the parameters available at trinityrock.com
When choosing a song, think about:

- Does it work for my voice?

- Are there any technical elements that are too difficult for me? (If so, perhaps save it for when you do the next grade)

- Do I enjoy singing it?

- Does it work with my other songs to create a good set list?

SONG 3: TECHNICAL FOCUS

Song 3 is designed to help you develop specific and relevant techniques in performance. Choose one of the technical focus songs from this book, which cover two specific technical elements.

SHEET MUSIC

If your choice for Song 2 is not from this book, you must provide the examiner with a photocopy. The title, writers of the song and your name should be on the sheet music. You must also bring an original copy of the book, or a download version with proof of purchase, for each song that you perform in the exam.

Your music can be:

- A lead sheet with lyrics, chords and melody line

- A chord chart with lyrics

- A full score using conventional staff notation

SINGING WITH BACKING TRACKS

All your backing tracks can be downloaded from soundwise.co.uk

- The backing tracks begin with a click track, which sets the tempo and helps you start accurately

- Be careful to balance the volume of the backing track against your voice

- Listen carefully to the backing track to ensure that you are singing in time

If you are creating your own backing track, here are some further tips:

- Make sure that the sound quality is of a good standard

- Think carefully about the instruments/sounds you are using on the backing track

- Avoid copying what you are singing in the exam on the backing track – it should support, not duplicate

- Do you need to include a click track at the beginning?

COPYRIGHT IN A SONG

If you are a singer, instrumentalist or songwriter it is important to know about copyright. When someone writes a song they automatically own the copyright (sometimes called 'the rights'). Copyright begins once a piece of music has been documented or recorded (eg by video, CD or score notation) and protects the interests of the creators. This means that others cannot copy it, sell it, make it available online or record it without the owner's permission or the appropriate licence.

COVER VERSIONS

- When an artist creates a new version of a song it is called a 'cover version'

- The majority of songwriters subscribe to licensing agencies, also known as 'collecting societies'. When a songwriter is a member of such an agency, the performing rights to their material are transferred to the agency (this includes cover versions of their songs)

- The agency works on the writer's behalf by issuing licences to performance venues, who report what songs have been played, which in turn means that the songwriter will receive a payment for any songs used

- You can create a cover version of a song and use it in an exam without needing a licence

There are different rules for broadcasting (eg TV, radio, internet), selling or copying (pressing CDs, DVDs etc), and for printed material, and the appropriate licences should be sought out.

YOUR
PAGE
NOTES

YOUR
PAGE
NOTES

YOUR
PAGE
NOTES